PRAISE for *Hip*

"With Camille's fantastic new book, *Hippiebanker*, you will find great, practical and simple tools to transform your work environment into the place it deserves to be!"

–GABRIELLE BERNSTEIN, *New York Times* Best Selling author of *Miracles Now*

"This is one of those rare books that actually contains wisdom."

– H. PALMER, author of the *Avatar Materials*

"Loved this book! It's not just for bankers or hippies, but for everyone that wants to bring peace and joy to their life and share it with others. The author's down-to-earth and humorous writing style made it fun to read. She encourages you to explore your spirituality and to find your own path to be a Lightworker . . .For me, the quote from Gandhi, summarizes the book: *Be the change you wish to see in this world.*" – LORA O'KELLY

"Camille has taken an idea—spirituality in the workplace—and redefined it. With her twelve-week plan, she makes it easy to bring love and understanding to a place where it is normally taboo. Simple in its design, let her lead you on a ride that will no doubt forever change your life and all those who come in contact with you." – DIANNE CAPLIN, author of *Gabbie Flowers and the Key to the Universe*

"Using the exercises contained in Hippiebanker encouraged me to approach my own work with an open heart and a desire to impact

those around me in a more conscious and meaningful way. You don't need to be adept at meditation or have advanced experience with any particular spiritual background in order to implement the simple and easy-to-follow teachings in this book. Excellent for both the beginner and the sage, *Hippiebanker* reminds you to have the courage to spread the Light wherever you are."

– NICHOLAS PEARSON Author of *Crystal Teachings*

"As if a switch was flipped, I will never again think of work the same way. It is not something to endure, counting the days till the weekend, but rather an experience to grow by bringing positivity to the world and enriching our souls in the process. Thank you *Hippiebanker* for opening my eyes and enriching my life."

–TINA GALVIN

"This guide has been a real eye-opening experience for me . . . Each week brought me to a clearer awareness of myself. 'What Am I Being?' . . . By week seven I found myself being lighter, more pleasant, more focused and productive. The guide has had a profound effect on my every day interactions with everyone around me." –FRANCINE LLERENA

"For those of you who are on a spiritual journey but find it challenging at times to stay on that journey at work, Hippiebanker gives us the tools to do just that. With her mixture of humor and groovy instructive writing, you'll find this a book that you'll continue to go back to for spiritual guidance. *Namaste.*"

– JOANNE DEAN

HIPPIEBANKER

HIPPIEBANKER

Bringing Peace, Love and Spirituality
to the Workplace

A 12-Week Guide to Becoming a
SPIRITUAL ACTIVIST
in Your Little Corner of the World

CAMILLE SACCO

Six Degrees Publishing Group
Portland · Oregon
USA

For information please contact the publisher by email:
Publisher@SixDegreesPublishing.com

Six Degrees Publishing Group
5331 S.W. Macadam Avenue, Suite 258
Portland, Oregon 97239

ISBN: 978-1-942497-08-0

Ebook ISBN : 978-1-942497-09-7

U.S. Library of Congress Control Number
2015948317

Front Cover illustration: Emanuel Vinatoru
Editorial & Design Supervision: Denise C. Williams

Published in the United States of America
First Edition

Printed Simultaneously in the United States of America
The United Kingdom and Australia

1   3   5   7   9 10   8   6   4   2

For my daughters,
Arianna and Carissa

I love you more.

CONTENTS

PREFACE

Hey! It's me, Hippiebanker, and I'm on a mission to bring peace, love and spirituality to the workplace. Now you might be saying, you can't be a hippie *and* a banker—you can't believe in peace and love *and* work at a bank! Well, I'm here to tell you, *yes you can!* and I am.

Let me start by saying I've been on my own spiritual journey for the past 25 years or so, reading every self-help book I could get my hands on, from Deepak Chopra and Mike Dooley to Neale Donald Walsch. Each book has brought me clarity, joy and abundance. They have brought me closer to a centered, well-balanced life and I consider each of those books to be personal treasures. However, the one area of my life I would like to enhance is my work life.

Now, if you were to start a conversation with someone

about bringing peace, love and spirituality to the workplace, I'm pretty sure they would get all *freaked out*. Love is not supposed to be in the workplace—there's no such thing. You go to work, do your job as best you can, and go home. There you can meditate, go to a yoga retreat, read self-help books and, hopefully, love your family. But bring that new age crap into the workplace? OH NO! It doesn't belong there.

Well, I'm here to tell you that's a bunch of malarkey! I'm here to tell you, it's OK to be a hippie and a banker. It's OK to believe in miracles and to believe love is all you need—and to bring that mindset into your workplace.

So who am I, and why am I writing this book? Before I go into my "professional credentials," you should understand my "hippie credentials."

I've been a hippie since I can remember. Born in 1960, I grew up listening to the Beatles. My cousin gave me the *Sgt. Pepper's Lonely Hearts Club Band* album when I was seven or eight years old, I became a Beatlemaniac before the age of ten, and I haven't looked back.

I vividly remember watching the movie, *A Hard Day's Night* and thinking about how much fun the Beatles seemed to be having. They were full of love, laughter and charm. There was one scene in particular that began a turning point in my life. In this scene, they escape from the television studio to a field outside and generally just let loose. They burst out of the building with the exclamation, "We're out!" and the song "Can't Buy Me Love" starts playing. Watching the Beatles playing on that field and cutting up made my heart sing. It made me think, it's OK to be yourself and be silly. It's OK to express yourself and not worry so much about fitting in or being like everyone else. It made me think, *I want to be that person that shines her light and allows others to light up.*

I truly believe "Love is all you need," which is my personal definition of what a hippie is. And as most hippies have done, I've attended several rallies throughout my years, all for one social cause or another. Recently, I was blessed with being one of the costume directors for a local production of the musical *Hair*, as well as being a cast member. That experience transformed me and solidified my mantra that I am and always will be a flower child.

In addition, I am currently a student of *A Course in Miracles*, and I am a certified, holistic life coach. I am also a certified Reiki practitioner. Spirituality is embedded in my bones!

And then there's work. I've been a banker/branch manager at a large financial institution for 15 years. I have opened four new branches and have been successful at each one. I have received numerous awards both in profitability as well as customer and employee experience. I have always led by "love" instead of "fear" and my employees have always been promoted in record time. I infuse spirituality in all my meetings and daily coaching sessions with my employees. My coworkers have had to listen to me talk about "putting it out in the Universe and setting your intentions for the day" for the past decade.

But it wasn't until I watched a video by *New York Times* bestselling author of the books *May Cause Miracles*, and *Spirit Junkie, a Radical Road to Self-Love and Miracles*, and the creator of "Spirit Junkie Master Classes," Gabby Bernstein, that I realized what my true purpose is. She talked about a banker-friend of hers who was feeling unfulfilled. She inspired him by telling him, "Your job is not to be the best banker or have the best spreadsheets. Your job is to go to work and *be the light* and bring forth your positive attitude. When you come to work with that intention, you allow others to light up and awaken to their authentic selves." It finally dawned on me what my calling is here on Earth: a *Lightworker!* My true purpose is to help light up my coworkers right from my desk at work—which is what I've been doing for the past 15 years.

That being said, I don't consider myself to be an expert on the subject of being a Lightworker. I just know I'm on a path to enrich my spirituality and bring it to all aspects of my life—and work is a big part of my life.

During the course of my career, I've incorporated all the lessons from this book into my daily plan, and I've noticed a visible shift in the vibrations at work, as well as an improvement in my own life. I've become much calmer at work, able to take on challenges with ease, and feel generally at peace with myself.

My ultimate goal in creating this guide is to help you lead through love, not fear, as well as help others on their spiritual journey. We are all leaders or mentors, regardless of our job title. Someone at work is looking up to you for advice and counsel.

Remember, you don't have to hold a position in order to be a leader.

~ *Camille Sacco*, Hippiebanker

INTRODUCTION

BEFORE WE GET STARTED, I would like to define and introduce a few concepts we'll be talking about in this book.

SPIRITUALITY

There is no single, widely-agreed upon definition of spirituality. The term can be applied to a wide variety of practices. Spirituality emphasizes ideas such as peace, love, compassion, patience, tolerance and forgiveness.

For the purposes of this book, spirituality is all of those paradigmatic ideas, including our quest for meaning in life and work. It's the search for feeling connected to other people and a higher being. Some people call that higher being God, the Universe, Spirit, Source, your inner guide and more. Spirituality, in the context of this book, is not religious in any way, however there is appreciation for all ministries.

LIGHTWORKERS

What is a Lightworker? I refer to this term often in this guide. According to Doreen Virtue, author of over 50 spiritual books over the past 25 years, "Lightworkers are those who have volunteered to help the planet and its population heal from the effects of fear."[1] They feel called to heal others through spirituality. To me, a Lightworker is also someone who wants to light up a room with their positive attitude and high vibrations. Simple enough.

SPIRITUAL ACTIVISTS

I quite often in this guide refer to being a "spiritual activist" at work. This term is really just combining Spirituality with Lightworker. Sometimes the word 'activist' scares people. It brings to mind young people protesting a cause and getting arrested for their shenanigans. This is not the case here. We just want to bring peace and love to the workplace, that's all.

MEDITATION

Throughout this book, I'll be encouraging you to meditate, especially in the morning before work. There are many meditations you can find—some are guided, some with music. Almost every popular self-help author has a recorded meditation CD. Find one that works for you. Some people like music and nature sounds. The idea is to spend quiet time in the morning, going past all the noise in your mind to that place where you can connect with your inner guide. Ask for guidance and you will be shown what to do. You'll be guided to your Highest Power. When you come out of meditation, feel that moment: Breathe in gratitude, breathe out love. Radiate. During the course of the day, you will discover you are better at decision making and able to handle stressful situations with ease.

> " *Spirituality is really just remembering we are all ONE.* "
> – Hippiebanker

The Plan & How to Use this Book

My intention is to start off with a weekly practice to help us tune in to a higher vibration and be in a state of JOY, which will in turn elevate our coworkers as well. This book is divided into 12 weekly lessons. There are pages at the end of each week to take daily notes. It works best if you read the chapter on a Sunday and commit to the practice for the workweek. Each weekly lesson will have a concept we'll be working on, along with a few intentions for that week. At the end of each day, I encourage you to write a few sentences about the lesson: What went well, what you would have done differently, what your strengths are and what opportunities exist. More than likely, by Friday (or whatever day your workweek ends) you will have gained some insight and had an AHA! moment or two. I'll begin each chapter with a recap of the previous week's lesson, and then dive in to the next lesson. I'm a firm believer in documenting your progress. This is your journal and I encourage you to track your thoughts, learning's and takeaways. Treat this like a training course at work. It's just not about graphs, balance sheets and revenue. We're talking serious stuff here!

In my career, all new beginnings have started with a mission statement. Let's make this ours:

Mission Statement

❧

I am here to lead and coach and be the light.
I am a Lightworker.
I accept that I am a spiritual activist at work,
and I decide right now that is my path.
I am stepping into my role.

❧

In every decision you make at work, come from a place of love. Think *what would love do?* and you won't go wrong.

JUMPING IN WITH A SAMPLE EXERCISE

TO TEST DRIVE THESE LESSONS, let's start with a very simple exercise. I've learned that it's always best to start at the beginning; and however small this first exercise may seem, I think it's the basis and foundation for a love-based workplace.

YOUR GOAL THIS WEEK:

Beginning this week, look into your coworker's eyes when talking to them and just SMILE.

You may think, *I already do that,* but I'm going to challenge you to pay attention to your actions, stay in the *now,* and really connect with your coworkers when you're having a conversation. I have to tell you, this one was difficult for me at first, and I have to really practice it to make it a habit. I know I don't look people in the eye. I get distracted and unfocused at times and forget to pay attention to the person I'm talking to. I can only imagine how that makes them feel. However, I'm on a mission and I'm committed to my lessons!

SETTING YOUR WEEKLY INTENTION:

Set your intention for this week and start each day with a meditation and an affirmation:

I choose to have a better conversation. I am a Lightworker.

Then, when you go to work, witness your thoughts and

behaviors and become conscious of what you are projecting onto your coworkers.

What is your face saying?

Are you frowning?

Are you deep in thought . . . are you distracted?

Be a witness to yourself, but don't be too judgmental. Just pay attention at first. Then, when you're ready, choose Love. Choose to look at your coworker with the mindset of, *I'm here for you. I'm here to listen. I'm here to help.* Look into their eyes and just smile. It's harder than you think. But if you practice, it will become second nature. Then watch what happens. Feel the energy in the room shift. It becomes lighter, more relaxed, and a much healthier environment.

This week is our introduction, just to get you in the groove. Take some mental notes during the week and get ready to join me for 12 weeks of fun and informative spiritual guidance.

WHY AM I SO PASSIONATE?

IN THE NOT-SO-DISTANT PAST, I thought I was going to change the world—we all did. Somehow along the way, we ended up in our current jobs and forgot who we were. I believe we don't need to quit our corporate job, move upstate and start an organic farm to show we are relevant. We can still leave a legacy. I believe there's more to work than just a place to make money and survive; it's a place where we can create and connect with our coworkers and at the same time elevate each other and raise the vibration in the room.

Let's start by committing to a 12-week plan to bring peace, love and spirituality to the workplace. Won't you join me in becoming a spiritual activist in your little corner of the world?

Remember . . . we are all one.
Namaste'

Week 1

Be Still and Listen

WE JUST FINISHED OUR FIRST sample exercise of bringing peace, love and spirituality into the workplace, which was to simply smile and look into our coworker's eyes when talking. Not a creepy kind of "I'm gazing into your eyes" look, but more like, "I'm really paying attention and I'm here for you" kind of look. Hopefully you didn't scare anyone this week.

How did you do?

Did you connect with someone?

Did you recognize that oneness?

It was a little unsettling for me at first. I was thinking, *Are you looking at my wrinkles? Is my mascara smudged?* Then when I got past my ego, it was kind of cool. I felt like I really connected on a soul level. After a while, it became second nature. I noticed I became calmer towards the end of the week, naturally holding people's attention while looking into their eyes and genuinely smiling. By the way, I did have a coworker helping me smile all week. She witnessed when I wasn't and gave me a gentle reminder.

It's always good to have someone on your side cheering you on. So to everyone who has joined me this past week, congratulations! We've conquered the first step: Smiling. Now on to our first lesson.

~

As Lightworkers, we are in tune with the Universal life force that surrounds us and guides us. Our values include honesty, humility, compassion and oneness. We are here to light the way and awaken our coworkers. As I said in the Introduction, I think we have a hard time acknowledging that peace and love could be brought into the workplace, but I'm going to challenge that theory. That's where it's needed most—in our daily grind. The purpose of spirituality in the workplace is to reconnect our lives with a sense of meaning and purpose. And our first skill-set is going to be the meat and potatoes of *being one* with our coworkers.

Listening to Understand

Our biggest communication problem is that we do not listen to understand. We listen to reply. Good listeners don't just hear the words; they actually seek to understand the person. How many times do you listen to someone at work, just nod continuously so they can finish and you can say what *you* have to say? What's going through my mind is, *Hurry up and finish so I can get these words out of my mouth because I'll forget them in two minutes.* If we can just breathe, slow down and go out of our way to listen, it sends a powerful message to our peers: *I trust and respect you and I care what you think. I value what you're saying.* That can be easier said than done.

Then there's that pesky little work habit we call multitasking. We're reading emails, answering texts and talking to someone at the same time. Let's not lie—we all do it. And the best part is, we think the other person isn't even aware. Oh, they won't notice or they won't care if I just answer this text. Really? It sends the message, *I don't care what you're saying; it's not important to me. Right now, I just have to read this text.* If we could stop multi-tasking and be in the present moment, we will convey a message of *what you're saying really matters.*

Another aspect of spirituality is listening to our own inner guidance, which is the greatest source for making decisions. When you have a tough decision to make, try to be still, listen and meditate. Doing so will guide you to the right answer. Go within and listen to your inner voice.

I've found that meditating every morning before work centers and aligns me with my higher self. I think more clearly during the day and I'm able to allow my authentic self to come through. Meditating is the cornerstone of peaceful thinking.

∾

OUR INTENTIONS FOR THIS WEEK

We'll start this week with the three simple intentions below. Meditate on these thoughts in the morning and refer to them throughout the day, as needed. At the end of the day, spend some time reflecting and ask yourself whether you were able to accomplish these ideas. Jot down some notes on the pages that follow this chapter.

- What went well?
- What you would like to work on?

Continue this practice throughout the week. Don't be too hard on yourself if it takes some time to become proficient. Baby steps. Willingness is your first step and if you've got that, the rest will come naturally. Here are our intentions:

1. Be present. No distractions. Give your full attention and ask follow up questions for clarity. If you can't give your full attention, it's better to say something like: "Can we continue this conversation later?"

2. No multi-tasking. One thing at a time. Pay attention to your thoughts. Stay present and in the now. People can tell when you've checked out and aren't listening anymore. You're not fooling anyone!

3. Listen to your inner guidance system. Set time aside in the morning to meditate focusing on these intentions and end the meditation with the affirmation: Today I will listen to understand.

I will leave you with a quote from the Dalai Lama: "When you talk, you are only repeating what you already know. But when you listen, you many learn something new."

Remember . . . we are all one.
Namaste'

Note: Five journal pages—one for each workday—are included for your use at the end of this and every weekly chapter. Each contains a quote or affirmation. This week's reflections center around listening.

*One of the most sincere forms of respect is actually
listening to what another has to say.*
– Bryant McGill

The word LISTEN contains the same letters
as the word SILENT.
– Alfred Brendel

Be still and listen. The earth is singing.
– Anonymous

People don't always need advice.
Sometimes all they really need is
a hand to hold, an ear to listen, and
a heart to understand them.

– Anonymous

Your profession is not what brings home your weekly paycheck. Your profession is what you're put here on earth to do, with such passion and such intensity that it becomes spiritual in calling.

– Vincent Van Gogh

WEEK 2

LET SOMEONE ELSE SHINE

WELCOME BACK! I HOPE YOU ENJOYED the first full week of your transformation into a spiritual activist at work. I also hope you took lots of notes and had several takeaways. As you continue this book, remember to review the first few weeks so you can watch your progress. Last week we focused on our listening skills and we committed to three intentions:

1. Being present, no distractions and to fully listen without talking.
2. Not multi-tasking. Paying attention to our thoughts and to the person in front of us.
3. Listening to our inner guidance system.

How did you do?

Did you get through the week without talking over a coworker?

I have to tell you, this has been a tough one for me. I've been known to interrupt on more than one occasion. For some reason, it's just so hard for me! I think it has something to do with the fact that I don't have a good memory and I forget what I'm going to say next so quickly. It's a work in process, and I can tell you, I'm not done with practicing this lesson—it will definitely be ongoing. However, when I began, I did see a small shift. I actually learned a thing or two when I remained quiet.

Remember, spirituality at work is all about being compassionate, finding a connection with your coworkers and also finding purpose in your work. What better way to do that than to listen to understand, rather than listen to reply?

Here's a tip I want to share that worked for me. I'm all about acronyms. They help me stay focused and grounded and they keep me in the present. When I found myself on the verge of interrupting, I said to myself: STOP IT! Which stands for: *Shhhh. The Other Person Is Talking.* Just saying this little tidbit to myself kept me from blurting out my agenda. Try it next time and see how it goes.

Now as far as listening to my own inner guidance system, I meditate daily. It's become part of my morning routine. Five minutes in the morning sets me up for my daily intention. You can also meditate at work. It's really not that difficult. Just go somewhere quiet for a few minutes and shut down. Close your eyes and disengage from work. Trust me, you only need a few minutes. It's like rebooting your computer. You'll feel recharged and energized!

Now, on to this week's lesson:

CHECK YOUR EGO AT THE DOOR

I HAVE TO SAY here, when I was writing this week's lesson, I woke up at 3 a.m. with a clear message from my inner guide. I heard loud and clear "IT'S NOT ABOUT YOU" . . . *hmmmm.*

Here's the thing: I went to sleep worrying about this book. I worry whether my message is clear and whether it's "too out there" for some people. I worry and think, *who am I to write a book like this?* After I heard this message and thought about it, this became crystal clear: *It's not about me. It's about the message.* I'm on a mission to start the conversation around bringing peace, love and spirituality to the workplace. I am very passionate about this subject and I try and live it every day. Who cares if I'm not a famous author or have any fancy credentials? As long as people are hearing this and are moved by the message, that's all that matters.

So that's my ego being checked at the door first and foremost.

On to applying this lesson to the workplace. Whether you've been with your company 20 years or just started yesterday, you can learn something new from whoever you meet. Anyone can contribute to a situation or opportunities in the workplace. I think what happens is the old dog doesn't want to learn new tricks or the young whippersnapper is not going to listen to the old fogey. Egos clashing!

Sometimes getting feedback from employees or coworkers puts us on the defense. We become enraged and the ego wants to fight back. Do your best to remain calm and listen to understand. If we just listen to each other, we open our minds to new and alternative possibilities and can channel our energy towards a better solution. But it takes practice—and patience!

> **" You didn't just magically land in your current role. Someone, somewhere, helped you."**
> – Hippiebanker

THINK ABOUT IT. You are where you are in your career only through the help of other people. You didn't just magically land in your current role. Someone, somewhere, helped you. Whether you're the old dog or the young whippersnapper, be that person who helps your coworker without your agenda coming into play. This week we are going to work on putting our ego on the back burner and allowing the Universe to guide us.

OUR INTENTIONS FOR THIS WEEK

1. Approach people and situations with curiosity. No matter your position in the company, you can learn something from everyone you meet. Be humble; and when you do learn something new, don't be afraid to say, "I didn't

know that. Thanks for the tip!" or something like that. Watch
the other person's face. They will undoubtedly light up!

2. Show by your actions "We are all on the same team."
Each person on the team is important. Whatever you do in
your career, be the best at it.

There was a time when I was a lunch lady at a middle
school; and, dammit, I was the best lunch lady in that
cafeteria. You can't run the company by yourself. All job-
families are important. Respect each team member, and you
will all succeed.

3. When credit is due, don't be the first to claim it. Stop and
let a coworker take credit for a group project. Remember,
it's a team effort most of the time. Let someone else shine
and watch what happens. It's amazing how much you can
accomplish when you don't concern yourself with who gets
credit for the idea.

～

STARTING MONDAY, just witness your ego and how it likes
to sabotage or take control of people and situations. Don't
be too judgmental with yourself. Just allow yourself to step
outside of yourself and be a gentle witness. Write in your
journal what you see and feel.

Then, on Tuesday start your practice.

Remember, this book's purpose is to help you become
a spiritual activist in your little corner of the world. It takes
time, so please document your progress on the following
pages, so you can refer to them often.

Practice . . . patience . . . practice . . . patience. It's the mantra of my life!

I will leave you with a quote from someone who knows a thing or two about business, Oprah Winfrey: "Check your ego at the door and check your gut instead. Every right decision I have ever made has come from my gut. Every wrong decision I've made was the result of me not listening to the greater voice of myself"

Remember . . . we are all one
Namaste'

Too much ego will kill your talent.
– Anonymous

Nothing kills the ego like playfulness, like laughter.
When you start taking like as fun, the ego has to die;
it cannot exist anymore.

– Osho

*Happiness blooms in the presence of
self-respect, and the absence of ego.*
– Jonathan Lockwood Huie

Don't lose hope, just lose your ego with work and patience.

– Anonymous

Leadership is not a popularity contest;
it's about leaving your ego at the door.
The name of the game is to lead without a title.
– Robin S. Sharma

WEEK 3

I THINK I'M FUNNY

HELLO FELLOW LIGHTWORKERS! Welcome to Week 3. I hope you are enjoying this 12-week plan and are taking lots of notes. The first few weeks can be very enlightening and I think you will find journaling to be very helpful in your progress.

Last week our mission was to "check your ego at the door." We approached people and situations with curiosity and showed by our actions that we are all on the same team.

How did you do?

Were you able to witness your ego trying to take control?

Were you able to let a coworker shine and take credit for a group project?

Well I hate saying this out loud, but when I first tried this exercise, I totally did *not* check my ego at the door. My ego came out with guns blazing! I hope you made progress this past week and made up for my lack of self-control.

Occasionally, we just have one of those weeks, and by golly, it's hard to continue to be the Light. It's tough when your ego sneaks up and gives you a punch in the gut. I will be the first to tell you, it's not easy to stay on the spiritual path. Sometimes we veer off, and head down a dark path. But I also will be the first to tell you that you can get right back on track. You don't have to continue down that dark road. Being a spiritual activist means waking up every day with the intention to bring your positive vibes to work. It's almost impossible to stay at that high frequency 100% of the time. What matters most is recognizing *when* we veer off track and having the ability and desire to get right back on the path.

> " *You can readjust and bring yourself back to a place of Love.* "
> – Hippiebanker

Sometimes, all hell breaks loose at work and you start hearing that little voice inside you saying, "I don't want to be the Light any more. Someone else do this. I can't!" When that happens, I suggest you, first and foremost, forgive yourself. You are on a journey to enlighten your own soul as well as others. This takes small, daily, practical steps, and it's not always easy. You will fall off the path, and I want you to know it's OK. You can start fresh tomorrow. You can readjust and bring yourself back to a place of love. I've learned that as long as you are willing to choose love over fear (the ego), you can get back on track. That willingness will allow you to step out of your thoughts and witness your behavior. If it doesn't serve you, choose again. The more you continue this practice of choosing again, the easier it will be.

Here are three steps I take when I've fallen off the spiritual path:

* **Go somewhere and just scream, vent, let loose.** It's best to get it out so those bad vibes don't cling to you, Try and do this away from your coworkers. I actually take a walk around the building and shake it off, like a duck. It works for me.

* **Find your happy place.** It could be your social media pages with positive affirmations, your self-help books or maybe there's that one book you continue to return to and re-read for support and guidance. Get back in the groove by remembering who you are. I find reading blogs and watching videos by my spiritual gurus, such as Gabby Bernstein and Doreen Virtue, to be a tremendous source of joy for me. Whenever I start to veer off, reading their work brings me back to my center.

* **Phone a friend.** Call your BFF (best friend forever), vent if you have to, and have a good laugh. Hopefully you have someone who will be there for you in good times and bad. Don't feel badly about calling them when you need to. They want and expect you to

reach out. If they are a true friend, they will help you get back on your feet. I am blessed to have a best friend here in Florida and a BFF of 40 years who lives in New York. I have a sister who is always there for me, as well as the most wonderful mother in the world who is the epitome of love. They have all laughed and cried with me and I wouldn't trade them in for the world.

I will tell you, sometimes the ego has its place and is necessary. Your ego may have helped you get to where you are today at work. I'm just saying don't let your ego get in the way. If it does, try these steps and continue to spend some time each morning meditating. A few minutes in the morning contemplating your day, envisioning what you would like it to look like and setting your intention for the day will set you up for success. It will keep you centered and balanced, and your Light will be shining once again.

Now on to this week's lesson. You'll like this one!

LET'S BRING FUN INTO THE WORKPLACE

FIRST, I'll ask you this:

Do you enjoy going to work?

Do you laugh at work?

Do you bring in your own brand of humor there?

Or . . .

Do you just go in, do your job, make small talk and go home?

I don't know about you, but God forbid, I'm not amusing

myself nor amusing my coworkers. I think I'm funny! However, it must be stated that I am not advocating your workplace be turned into *Romper Room* or *Barney and Friends*. There's a time for play and a time to work hard. I believe we need to get the balance right and ensure we build in some fun time that is appropriate and not distracting from our daily work. If you choose to have a positive attitude and embrace enthusiasm and fun, you will directly affect the vibe in the room and it will rub off on your coworkers. Don't discount the importance of fun in the workplace.

Spirituality at work is all about connecting with other people, and what better way to connect is there than to laugh? I can tell you this: When you're in a leadership or mentor role, and employees are having fun and laughing, there's a better vibe, better conversations, and you will see *better results*. Happy employees are more creative and they will bring forth their best energy to the team. Your job as a leader or mentor is to make sure your employees are happy, productive and having fun. No joke.

In my opinion, the easiest way to bring fun into the workplace is to *just be you*. Allow your true spirit to shine through and watch what happens. Don't worry about being corporate or politically correct all the time. Let everyone see who you really are. Joke around and be that person that everyone is drawn to. You'll lighten the room, and guess what? Research shows that employees are more productive and do their best work in an environment that allows them to be relaxed and at peace.[2]

So this week, let's play hooky and have fun. Go into work with the mindset of "I'm here to bring joy, laughter and a joke or two." See how many coworkers you can make smile. Make it your mission to bring forth that positive attitude and throw a little humor in the mix.

I will never forget the time when I left one position to go to another and one of my employees said to me "Now who am I going to laugh with every day?" That was probably the best going away message I could have heard.

All the world wants is your authentic self. Approach this workweek with a wink and a smile. Your coworkers may think you're bonkers, but I'll bet they'll laugh.

Our Intentions for This Week

1. Request interesting trivia facts about each coworker. Write each fact on a slip of paper, fold up and put in a basket. Each day take one or two out during a meeting or lunch gathering and see who can match the fact with the employee. Give a prize at the end of the week to the employee who knows the most about his/her coworkers.

2. Have an employee appreciation week. If you have a bulletin board or white erase board at work, pick one employee or coworker each day and write their name at the top. Ask each coworker to write a sentence about that person and why they are special or what they like best about that person.

3. Pot luck Friday. Everyone loves food. Pick a theme lunch for Friday and ask everyone to contribute a dish. Most employees are in a good mood on Friday. A fun lunch makes a pleasant end to the week.

If you have any ideas, I encourage you to implement them. Make this week fun for you and for your team. Happy employees = Happy customers = Better bottom line.

And for the record, you can be spiritual and have a great sense of humor. It is possible!

Remember . . . we are all one
Namaste'

To make customers happy, we have to
make sure our employees are happy first.
– Tony Hsieh, CEO of Zappos

*You can build a much more wonderful company
on love than you can on fear.*
– Kip Tindell, The Container Store

When you lavish praise on people, they flourish. Criticize, and they shrivel up.

– Richard Branson, Virgin Group

You have to be a place that's more than a
paycheck for people.
– Rick Fererico, P.F. Chang's

If you are lucky enough to be someone's employer,
then you have a moral obligation to make sure people
do look forward to coming to work in the morning.
– John Mackey, Whole Foods Market

Be the Change

Hello everyone! I hope you had a great week filled with fun! Did your coworkers wonder what got into you? I hope they were amused. I always make it a point to have fun at work.

Now, I know I have work to accomplish, and by all means, I get my work done; however, I always throw some humor in the mix. It makes the day go by quicker when employees are laughing and having fun. And guess what? When employees are laughing and smiling, they will enjoy their work and it will show. They'll whistle while they work. And, they will turn around and smile at the customers. Take a moment to really laugh with your teammates right before a customer walks in the door or right before they have a call to make. You will visibly see a shift in their demeanor when they approach that customer. It will be warm and inviting.

What a great employee and customer experience!

Now, back to work and on to this week's lesson:

WHAT ARE YOU BEING AT WORK?

THERE'S A DIFFERENCE between being and doing. So my question to you is, *what are you being at work?* Not what are you doing, not what is your title nor what is your profession. Ask yourself these questions:

How am I leading?

What words am I using?

Do I check for clarity?

Do I engage, versus dictate?

Look in the mirror. What face am I bringing to work? Don't judge yourself. Don't let your ego judge your ego. Instead, witness your behaviors and think about the question:

What am I BEING?

In the Introduction to this guide, I suggested, *you can be a hippie and a banker.* Most people would not think that a banker could also be a spiritual activist. It really doesn't matter what you do in your life—you can bring Light to any job. It's about what you are being in that position.

A long time ago, when I started my first job, my dad told me, "Whatever job you do in life, be the best at it and you will rise to the top." I will never forget those words of wisdom. They have served me well.

Let's examine three "being" skills and break them down to how we can apply them to the workplace.

Our Intentions for This Week.

1. Empathy. Putting yourself in other people's shoes and being able to identify with them.

Ask yourself:

* Do I try to see things from a coworker's point of view?

When you do, you'll realize other people aren't intentionally being unreasonable. They're probably just reacting to a situation based on the knowledge they have. Once you see why they are coming from that standpoint, acknowledge it. Remember, acknowledgment does not always mean you are in agreement. Sometimes it means agreeing to disagree.

Next, examine your attitude about the situation:

* Are you more concerned with being right or winning the argument?

Or . . .

* Is it your priority to find a solution?

Remember to use those listening skills from Week 1.

2. Approachable. In other words, being warm and inviting. Are your coworkers comfortable coming to you for advice, direction or help?

Here are some questions to ask yourself:

* Does my posture indicate I don't mind being approached?
* Do I turn to face my coworker when they talk to me?
* Do I make it a point to make eye contact during the Monday morning meeting?

* Can my coworkers find me during the day or do I shut myself in an office behind a door, tapping away on the computer?

If you are in a leadership position, I encourage you to be out and about and available to your team. When you do so, I guarantee they will see you as approachable. Most employees are self-sufficient and just want to know they can count on their supervisor to be available if they need them.

3. Mindfulness. Paying attention in a particular way, on purpose, in the present moment, and non-judgmentally.

How can you tell if you're mindful? You can hear yourself think. You are open to new ideas. Your thoughts are clear. The best way I've found to be mindful is to meditate every morning. (Yes, again—meditate!)

There are a variety of meditations you can find. Some are guided meditations, others with music. Some people are drawn to music, others to nature sounds. Almost every popular self-help author has a recorded meditation. Find one that works for you. The idea is to spend quiet time in the morning, going past all the noise in your mind to that place you can connect with your inner guide. Ask for guidance and you will be shown what to do. You'll be guided to your highest power. When you come out of meditation *feel that moment*, breathe in gratitude, breathe out love. Radiate. During the course of the day you will discover you will be better at decision making and able to handle stressful situations with ease.

Of course, you'll get caught up in the constant distractions at work. That's a given. The trick is to come back from the distractions and use your "being" skills. One tip I use is to have a reminder set on my phone at noon. It says "Be the Light." It's a reminder to check in on myself: *What are you being?* It brings me to that moment and reminds me to stay in the present. Try it!

At the end of your day, *ask yourself:*

* Is my workplace better because I showed up today?

Take lots of notes this week and try to answer some of these questions. Be honest with yourself and evaluate your progress. And when people start to notice a difference in you and say things like "you've changed." Tell them, *I didn't change. I just woke up!*

Remember . . . we are all one
Namaste'

Your job is not to judge. Your job is not to figure out if someone deserves something. Your job is to lift the fallen, to restore the broken, and to heal the hurting.

– Joel Olsteen

*I think we all have empathy. We may not have
enough courage to display it.*

– Maya Angelou

Patient and approachable mentors can bring
seemingly impossible goals down to earth
and give those they advise a shot of confidence.

– Rodd Wagner and Jim Hartner

Mindfulness helps you go home to the present.
And every time you go there and recognize a condition of
happiness that you have, happiness comes.

– Thich Nhat Hanh

Give a damn. Many damns. More damns than anyone
– Dale Partridge

Week 5

PROJECT A SPIRIT OF LIGHT

HELLO FELLOW ACTIVISTS! Last week, we asked the question, "what are you *being* at work?" not, "what you are doing?" There's a difference. Doing is busy-work. Being is internal. The being skills we talked about last week were empathy, being approachable and mindfulness.

Let's start with empathy. Did you have a chance last week to put yourself in a coworker's shoes? This situation could come up quite often if you are in an office environment with a lot of different personalities. It takes being deliberate in your thoughts and actions to practice empathy. I hope you had the chance to practice that "being" skill.

Now, being "approachable" might take a little time. You might need to practice that for more than a week. This particular concept took me a while to learn. At first, my ego kept sneaking around the corner, telling me, "In order to be a strong leader, you have to be stern and lead through fear." If you've had a stern supervisor like that, you know how it feels. Continue to practice being approachable if this is an area of needed improvement for you.

Finally, we practiced mindfulness—really paying attention in a particular way and on purpose. Mindfulness is *being in the now.* Thoughts are clear and you can make better decisions.

～

So, how did you do? Did you try meditating? My morning meditations have become routine for me, and I can tell you I feel off during the day if I don't take time to meditate. Being mindful really takes you out of the fog you've been living in and brings you to the here and now. When you are in the now, you can really connect with your coworkers. And that's what spirituality at work is all about—providing feelings of understanding and feeling connected to our coworkers. It's a desire to be of service to other people and make a difference with our actions. It is demonstrated by compassion and our topic for this week:

CARING

I WAS WATCHING A VIDEO recently about branding a product and how to sell it. The woman in the video came up with this brilliant idea: "How about we try to show the customer we care?" Before I knew it, I blurted out to the TV, "How about we DO care?!"

A famous quote I refer to when coaching employees

is, "People don't care about how much you know, until they know how much you care." If we want to inspire others, this is a very important truth. Sometimes at work we get wrapped up in what we are *doing* and forget what we are *being*. When you focus on others, a miraculous thing happens . . . you see things differently, and you begin to care. If you want to be effective in communicating your ideas to others, show you care. If you want to get your point across, show you care. There's a catch though: You have to *really* care. Not just "try to show" you care, like the person in the video. *Genuinely care.* Coworkers, employees and customers can sense when you truly care about them, versus someone who just "talks the talk." All the skills and education in the world won't impress anyone as much as good old-fashioned caring.

OUR INTENTIONS FOR THIS WEEK

1. Get to know your coworkers. How do you know about them? You ask questions and actually stay focused when they answer. Try active listening on your part, and when you find that '*me too!*' moment, you'll be connected. I've done many workshops on connecting with customers and finding that '*me too!*' moment. Funny enough, it also applies to our coworkers.

Try this exercise: Start asking basic questions about family, friends, where they grew up, favorite vacations spots, and so forth. It won't take more than five questions before you find common ground. Then the walls come down and you are connected!

We all long for a feeling of being home and being one with another. That familiarity makes us feel warm and comforted.

2. Walk the walk and do what you say. We've all had supervisors and coworkers who can dish out orders, however somehow it doesn't apply to them. If you say you are going to do something, do it. Don't just say it. Your actions will go a long way and will show you care about your coworkers. An important lesson I learned from one of my mentors was this: *frequency of message.* Don't think one time will do the trick—remember to be consistent in your actions.

3. Apologize, even if you are not wrong. This one might be a hard pill to swallow for some. Believe it or not, it will make you feel better and there will be a better vibe in the room. Apologies show you care more about your coworker than winning an argument. Apologies can break down barriers in an instant. This one might not come up often at work, but if it does be prepared.

Regardless of your title in any given profession, you are probably trying to engage, connect and communicate with your coworkers and/or employees. People are not going to listen to you until they genuinely feel you care about them. When they truly know, then they will care about you as well. They will listen and do anything for you. But you have to be genuine. Be authentic and stand out from the crowd.

❧

SPIRITUALITY AT WORK is about people seeing work as a spiritual path and an opportunity to grow and contribute to society in a meaningful way. It's about care, compassion and support of others. Be true to yourself and others.

One thing I would like to add here. Truly caring about our coworkers and employees sometimes involves tough love. If we truly care, sometimes we have to deliver critique and constructive criticism.

If you are a leader, it is not in your employee's best interest to brush aside any coaching sessions that could come up during the day. Some supervisors do not like conflict and will not address any issues or concerns with an employee's performance. I disagree. The best way to help an employee succeed and grow with the company is to be honest and give continuous direct feedback. Shine the light on any issues, have an open dialogue about situations or concerns in a constructive manner, and that will undoubtedly show you care.

Most people come to work to do their best. If you want to show you care, help people get to the next level by addressing any concerns you see. True leaders do not shy away from difficult situations—they learn from them. Just come from a place of love and you won't go wrong.

I may be saying something that sounds simplistic to you: Care about the people you work with. It's not hard, but it does take a conscious effort on your part. Think of this as *organic growth.*

This is an important message to keep sharing. If we all

are to become spiritual activists in our own little corner of the world, we need to continue to spread the message with our coworkers and the people we come in contact with on a daily basis. We share a responsibility for creating a warm and inviting workplace. We can either project a *Spirit of Light* or a spirit of shadow. We have a choice. A leader takes responsibility for what he or she is projecting. *Be the Light!*

Remember . . . we are all one.
Namaste'

Never believe that a few caring people can't change the world. For, indeed, that's all who ever have.
– Margaret Mead

Nobody is ever too busy. If they care, they will make time.
– Anonymous

To make a difference in someone's life, you don't have to be brilliant, rich, beautiful or perfect. You just have to care.
– Mandy Hale

*Even the smallest act of caring for another person
is like a drop of water—it will make ripples
throughout the entire pond.*

– Jessy & Bryan Matteo

The best and most beautiful things in the world cannot be seen or even touched. They must be felt with the heart.
– Helen Keller

WEEK 6

I Can See Your Aura Glowing

LAST WEEK'S LESSON was about showing our coworkers we care about them. Not just, "Hey, how was your weekend? Great, me too, let's get started on this week's project," but really getting to know our coworkers, who they are and what makes them tick—being authentic and genuinely caring.

So how did you do? Did you learn a thing or two about someone? Did you find that "me too!" moment when you really connected? Did you find out there really are only six degrees of separation?

I bet it didn't take long to find common ground with a coworker when you began to ask questions and got to know them. It's kind of awesome to feel like you're one with someone, and it makes work more pleasant. The vibration in the room is elevated and people smile more often too. I know when I find that common ground with a coworker, I can't wait to go to work and share stories. You might also learn something new. How cool is that?

Now on to this week's lesson:

～

Whether you are in a leadership position or not, there is usually someone at work you can mentor or coach. People will look up to you if you have their best interest at heart. Everyone goes to work seeking to put their best foot forward, and we all need a little recognition just to ensure we are on the right path and that our efforts mean something.

Now, when you see someone stepping up their game, you can always say to them "good job!" or "job well done." Those are the obvious words you would use when you want to compliment someone. I'm going to take it a step further: When you see someone going above and beyond and accomplishing a task at work, tell that person:

I'm Proud of You!

To be proud of someone means you know where they've been and how far they've come. Pride is essentially a word about growth. It's imperative to remember this: "I'm proud of you" must come from someone who's been in their shoes—from someone who has been in their position. Show you've been there, you see how hard that person has worked and can see their accomplishments. Make sure you make it meaningful and specific. I think the key is, you don't want to sound condescending. Don't forget, everyone is on a different path. Some people are quick learners; some need a little more time. Acknowledge small shifts in behavior, as well as full-blown accomplishments. I believe everyone comes to work to do his or her personal best. When you say, "I'm proud of you," it means you admire them and they've made a big achievement. It's positive reinforcement and it means you care about them and seeing them succeed.

Being proud of someone is about connection, shared history and growth. If spirituality at work is about connection, then expressing "I'm proud of you" is choosing love by choosing to show your love and allowing others to shine. Little by little, you can help unblock their fears and help your coworkers and employees grow, which will allow their Light to shine brighter. I can tell you from personal experience when one of my mentors told me "I'm proud of you" all distractions melted away and I felt like I was ready to take on the world. I felt the love coming through the phone, even though it wasn't in person.

In addition to being proud of an employee or coworker, be proud of yourself. For some people, this is not an easy task. It doesn't feel right to acknowledge your own achievements. It feels like you're being self-absorbed. If you are feeling that way, I'll say this: *Knock it off!* You can't spread the love if you don't love yourself first. This took me a long time to accept, as I kept hearing my inner voice tell me "Who do you think you are?"

This year, I've started reading the lessons in *A Course in Miracles*. I've found this book to be extremely complex, yet insightful. While reading the book, it actually becomes an experience for me. The basic teaching of this book is that the "way to love and inner peace is through forgiveness." In another profound and must-read book *A Return to Love,* the author, Marianne Williamson, shares her reflections on *A Course in Miracles.* Whenever I start to doubt myself about my real job or mission in life, I refer to this quote from Marianne:

> *Our deepest fear is not that we are inadequate. Our deepest fear is that we are powerful beyond measure. It is our Light, not our darkness that most frightens us. We ask ourselves, who am I to be brilliant, gorgeous, talented and fabulous. Actually, who are you not to be?*[3]

OUR INTENTIONS FOR THIS WEEK

1. Look for opportunities to tell someone you're proud of them. Even small accomplishments should be acknowledged. If you have an employee who is struggling with a seemingly small task, make sure you notice any improvement. One side note: Please make sure it is not random and used too often. I would try and coach someone throughout the week and when you see a definite improvement in a skill, tell them you're proud of them. Say it once and say it with meaning. Remember to come from a place of love and smile. Even if it's through the phone, your smile will come shining through.

2. Don't forget to be proud of yourself. Be proud of yourself for taking this journey and committing to become a spiritual activist in the workplace. This is no easy task and it takes determination, consistency and tenacity. Do not doubt for a minute your commitment. When your ego starts sneaking in, which it will, tell it this: "Take a back seat. I don't have time for this small-minded way of thinking. I've got to help heal the world from my desk at work and make a difference!"

3. Take time this week for some self-care. Give yourself a pat on the back and indulge in a little "me" time. Whatever you enjoy doing, whether it be taking a bath, listening to music, or walking in the park, make time for it. If you feel good about yourself, you'll undoubtedly radiate and have an abundance of love to give. Never underestimate the importance of self-love.

So, this week try it. Tell someone you're proud of him or her. It feels amazing to have someone support you and raise you up. You'll see people perk up, stand taller, and secretly smile. You might even see their aura glow brighter! I've noticed a shift in the energy at work and positivity exploding everywhere. Remember, it's about small, organic growth. Take time for yourself as well this week. You've come a long way, baby. And take time to reflect by reading your notes from the past few weeks.

I'll bet you've learned a thing or two since we first started on our journey. Hey, you've got this. And just so you know, *I'm proud of you!*

Remember . . . we are all one
Namaste'

Anyone who ever gave you confidence, you owe them a lot.
– Truman Capote, *Breakfast at Tiffany's*

The privilege of a lifetime is being who you are.
    – Joseph Campbell

I hope you live a life you're proud of. If you find that you are not, I hope you have the strength to start all over again.
– F. Scott Fitzgerald

Be strong, but not rude. Be kind, but not weak.
Be bold, but not bully. Be humble, but not timid.
Be proud, but not arrogant.

– Zig Ziglar

Define success on your own terms, achieve it by your own rules, and build a life you're proud to live.

– Anne Sweeney

WEEK 7

SPRINKLE WITH LOVE

HELLO EVERYONE. LAST WEEK we talked about telling a coworker you're proud of them. In order to be proud of someone, you have to in some way walked in their shocs or "been there" and can, therefore, see how much they have accomplished. Only then you can say "I'm proud of you" because, as we learned last week, pride is about *connection*, shared history and growth.

So, were you able to say those words? I did, and you know what? My thoughts were spot on. People actually perk up, straighten up and just beam. It's a great feeling for you, your coworker or employee, and there is definitely a higher vibe in the room. I'd say it's super cool. I hope you, also, took some time to acknowledge your commitment to this journey and reflect on how far you've come.

Do you feel you are making a difference at work?

Can you feel the air starting to clear and work becoming a pleasant place to spend your day?

If you are following these guidelines, I hope you are seeing a difference. We are at our halfway point and I would like you to take a moment and say out loud "I'm proud of myself." Now on to this week's lesson:

～

WE'VE BEEN FOCUSING on being a Lightworker and enlightening others with our positive energy, right? When you come to work with the attitude of "I'm here to be the Light," regardless of your actual job title, you bring a positive energy to anything you do, and in turn, you allow others to light up. I can tell you this: I'm going to work thinking I can awaken everyone at once. "OK everyone, I'm on this spiritual path; it's great; you're gonna love it. Come on everyone! Join me in the parade!"

> **"Slow down! This isn't a marathon. Everything happens in divine time."**
> – Hippiebanker

Well it kind of hit me this week . . . they aren't all as enthused as I am. My usual sunshine self isn't working as fast as I would like it to. So, I meditated one morning and asked for clarity. I asked the Universe "What is my next step" and you know what message I got? *Slow down! This isn't a marathon. Everything happens in divine time.* This has been my problem my whole life, both personally and professionally. I get a concept or idea, and as soon as I have it, I expect everyone else to get it. It's not that I think I'm so special; it's quite the opposite. I got it, so of course, you should get it. Patience. That lesson of patience keeps coming around. So our lesson for this week is this:

START WITH ONE PERSON

PICK THE ONE PERSON at work who is in tune with you. The one who wants to know more about what spiritual, new age book you're reading, who seems interested when you tell them you're now a certified, Holistic Life Coach. Start talking to them about all the positive changes that are happening in your life and see if they are experiencing any similar shifts. Share your passion and encourage them to read a new book, take a new course online, and maybe visit a metaphysical store with you. Maybe even start a gratitude list. Come from a place of love, compassion and kindness within you and you'll have a *spiritual ally* at work that you can collaborate with. Nurture that one person, sprinkle with love and you'll see your coworker blossom into a beautiful butterfly.

OUR INTENTIONS FOR THIS WEEK

1. Don't try to change everyone at once. I made the mistake of preaching my newly found knowledge to everyone I met at work. I can tell you, it turned people off. If they aren't ready to receive your message, it just means they aren't there yet spiritually. Don't try and change the whole office at once—everyone is at a different stage, and you are not there to judge. Believe it or not, it's best to preach to the choir. They are already on a spiritual path and want to absorb more insight. They are ready, willing and able to join you in the crusade. Once you start with that one person, others will see you both shining your Light and want to join in on the fun. Believe me, when you are running around the office smiling, laughing and actually glowing, your coworkers are going to want to know what's gotten into you.

2. When you do find that one person, start off gently. Don't overload them with every book you've read and every new concept you're into. Ask questions about what they are learning and make sure it's a two-way street. Try not to turn this into a preaching session. You can learn something from every person you meet. Important reminder: *As you teach, you learn.*

3. When coworkers aren't as interest in your course of action as you would like them to be, don't be too harsh. One important lesson to remember is this: Try not to make your relationship with that one person "special." Your intention is not to start your own "club" and exclude others who aren't on the journey yet. Be mindful of how those you work with perceive your thoughts and actions. Your job as a Lightworker is to help others along the way—not to judge where someone is on their spiritual path. Be sensitive to your other coworkers' feelings. They may come around in their own time, just like we all did.

$\sim$

WE ARE ALL MEANT TO SHINE, and as we do, we allow others to do the same. Start with one person at work and slowly you'll see the whole office coming around. It's time to stop playing small and step into our role as Lightworkers. Whatever your profession, whatever job you do, whether you've worked your way up to CEO of a company or you're a teenager with your first part time job in college, you can still be the Light and shine on. I promise you, we can light up the world one person at a time.

I'll leave you with a task: Research Yogi Bhajan and the Five Sutras of the Aquarian Age. Yogi Bhajan brought Kundalini Yoga to the East in 1968, during the midst of the counter-culture revolution. He has inspired thousands of people as a spiritual teacher and yogi and his Five Sutras, are in my opinion, words to live by. We will be applying these sutras to the workplace in the next few chapters.

Remember . . . we are all one.
Namaste'

The world is changed by your example,
not by your opinion.
– Paul Coelho

Anyone that encourages intellectual, emotional, artistic or spiritual growth is worth keeping. Don't let them go.

– Anonymous

*You can preach a better sermon with your
life than with your lips.*

– Oliver Goldsmith

Let your faith be bigger than your fear.
  – Anonymous

*Once you awaken, you will have
no interest in judging those who sleep.*
– James Blanchard Cisneros

WEEK 8

REFLECTIONS OF YOU

HELLO FELLOW LIGHTWORKERS! Last week our lesson was to *start with one person*—the one at work who would like to join you on your path and further their awareness. As we continue on our spiritual journey and gain more insight, it's natural to want to share our stories and newfound knowledge with others. It's much easier preaching to the choir than it is to start a revolution, isn't it?

So, how did it go? Did you find your soul sister at work? I hope you did. If not, don't worry. As you continue on your journey, people will notice your inner peace and gradually want to know more about what you're doing. Then you can share your thoughts with them.

Now on to this week's lesson:

I LEFT YOU WITH A TASK last week to research "The Five Sutras of the Aquarian Age." I've been reading a lot about Yogi Bhajan, spiritual teacher and master of Kundalini Yoga. In his teachings, he shared five principles, which he called the Five Sutras of the Aquarian Age. Sutras are spiritual concepts reduced to one sentence, which are simple, yet deep and profound. They are literally words to live by. According to Yogi Bhajan, the Aquarian Age is here now.

The song, "Aquarius," from the 1967 Broadway musical, *Hair*, is the epitome of the Aquarian Age . . . "harmony and understanding, sympathy and trust abounding. No more falsehoods or derisions, golden living dreams of visions. Mystic crystal revelation and the minds true liberation." Now that's a mouthful! It's really just about the fact that "Peace will guide the planets and love will steer the stars." If you're a hippie like me, this is probably one of your favorite songs and one of your mantras in life.

Over the next five weeks we will be attempting to apply the Five Sutras to the workplace. We'll start with the first sutra which is:

RECOGNIZE THAT THE OTHER PERSON IS YOU

SO WHAT DOES "recognize that the other person is you" mean, and how can you apply it to your workplace? I believe it means that when you find yourself in a situation where you don't see eye-to-eye with someone else at work—whether it be your coworker, your boss or your employee—recognize that person is you. What you don't like about a situation or a person is actually a reflection of you, and has nothing to do with them. Before you get angry with that person, stop and meditate on the situation. Ask your inner guide, the Universe, why this situation came into being. People and situations come into your life as assignments. They are here to teach us and help us grow.

When we are in conflict with a situation or a person, it's usually in an area that we are still working on. We think we have it resolved; however, when we see it in another person, it brings to light the fact that it is still *unresolved within ourselves.* Whenever you decide to act on a fear-based impulse of not agreeing with a coworker, or causing a conflict, you are differentiating yourself from the other person and creating a separation.

So what does "creating a separation" mean? When we think we are special or above someone, or think someone else is special or above us, we have created a division between them and us. We have put ourselves or someone else on a pedestal, when really we are all the same. We are actually each other's mirrors. The other person actually reflects the shadow parts of our self.

When we can begin to grasp this concept and embrace it, we can then move into oneness. We can shine Light on the situation and move forward. We are no longer better or worse than our coworkers, our peers, our supervisor. We are all equal. Once we recognize this equality—this oneness—we can move from the mentality of *it's all about me* and start moving towards *we are all one.* It's more than just trying to see the other person's point of view; it's actually looking deeper and recognizing that the other person *is* you. When we can embrace this concept, all defenses come down. The walls between each other crumble and we can come from a place of love. It certainly is a much better work environment and the tension in the air dissipates. Now, mind you, not everyone is going to come to this realization quickly. Most people are accustomed to conflict at work and have dealt with it for years in their own way.

If you want change, you are going to have to start with yourself. As Gandhi said, "Be the change." Start a new way of thinking. It begins with you.

It's time to look in the mirror and be open to non-judgmental self-reflection.

It's time to have an honest conversation with yourself in order to better yourself so you can help others . . . and that's what we are here to do when we are committed to being a spiritual activist at work.

Our Intentions for This Week

1. When a situation arises where you don't see eye-to-eye with a coworker, try to remove yourself from the situation and go to quiet place. Before you allow your ego to take control, do a meditation or affirmation on clearing your throat chakra. We each have seven chakras, which simply put, are energy centers in our bodies through which energy flows.

Your throat chakra is the center that governs your

speech and expression. Ask the Universe to clear the way to allow you to speak your truth with ease and in a loving manner. Ask why is this situation coming into being and what am I here to learn? Ask how can I become one with this person? Your inner guide will lead you to the answer. Breathe and come from a place of Love.

2. Begin the process of moving from a *"me"* mentality to a *"we"* mentality. Reflect on why we put others on a pedestal or why we think we are above others. What qualities do they have that are lacking in you? Why do we think we are special? Begin to perceive others as our sisters and brothers who are on the same journey to enlightenment as we are. Some are farther along the path and some are struggling to catch up.

We are all ultimately headed in the same direction and to the same place. Just because some of us are farther along doesn't make that person better or worse. It's not a race. If you were struggling, I'm sure you would want someone to pick you up and help you on the path. A true leader stops to help those around them that have fallen and gets them back on their feet again.

3. Hold Some Space. Recently, I've read about the practice of "holding space" for someone. It's sitting with someone while they are going through a rough time and *not* trying to fix the problem, give advice or control the outcome. It's about allowing that person to be vulnerable and feel weak without fear of being judged. Thus, we open our hearts and offer unconditional love and support without judgment.

As for me, it's about time I learn this beautiful concept and try holding space for the people in my life that I truly care about, whether it be my family or my coworkers. I encourage you to read more about this concept and practice holding space this week.

While you practice being non-judgmental with your coworkers this week, don't forget to accept yourself for who you are. Be open and don't be afraid to show your own vulnerability. We are all spiritual teachers in some form or another. We each have a unique story to tell and if we can truly recognize the imperfections in each other and rise above them, we will begin to change the world. Take time this week to really reflect on the First Sutra. It's the groundwork for our next few weeks.

Don't lower your vibration when an unpleasant situation arises at work. Remember to let your love send off so much positive energy that it shifts the vibrations in the room.

I'll leave you with this quote from, of all things, a very profound walrus! "I am he as you are he as you are me and we are all together."

Remember . . . we are all one
Namaste'

The greatest act of courage is to be and own all that you are.
Without apology. Without excuses and without any masks
to cover the truth of who you truly are.

– Debbie Ford

Each person you meet is an aspect of yourself,
clamoring for love
– Eric Micha'el Leventhal

A flower does not think of competing with the flower next to it. It just blooms.

– Zen Shin

See the Light in others, and treat them
as if that is all you see.
– Dr. Wayne Dyer

Let's stop believing that our differences
make us superior or inferior to one another.
– Don Miguel Ruiz

SURRENDER . . . SURRENDER

WELCOME BACK FELLOW HIPPIES! Last week we talked about the Five Sutras of the Aquarian Age and we started with the First Sutra: *Recognize that the other person is you.*

Did you test it out at work and try to really connect with a coworker and come from a place of "we are all one?" If so, I bet it was a game changer.

Did you take some time to read about the seven chakras and how to clear the energies?

Did you read about "holding space" or practice this lovely idea?

The Five Sutras, as we learned last week, are spiritual concepts reduced to one simple, yet very profound and deep, sentence. I must admit, I continue to learn quite a bit from practicing them.

I'm also learning that the more you teach, the more

you learn. We all have our own stories to tell, and I believe, deep down, we are *all* spiritual teachers. I have had many encounters with coworkers, employees, customers and supervisors throughout the years. Some have been pleasant, fun and uplifting; others have been less than stellar. However, I can tell you this: I have learned something from everyone I've met. I've learned how to be a better boss, and I've also learned "I would never treat an employee like that!" All situations are opportunities for growth.

If you can be honest with yourself, lighten up, and not take yourself or others so seriously, you will realize that we are all beautifully imperfect. .

I hope you enjoyed last week's lesson as we are going to continue to learn about and apply the Second Sutra to the workplace, which is:

THERE IS A WAY THROUGH EVERY BLOCK

QUITE OFTEN AT WORK, we come across a block. We get stuck and we need help moving forward. There are all kinds of blocks we come across on a daily basis—big and small— with both people and situations. The computer crashes; a coworker calls in sick; you have an irate customer on the phone; or there's a deadline that seems impossible to meet.

Most of us will first stop, scratch our head, and then try to figure out how to get past this mountainous mess. We'll debate the pros and cons of how to proceed. Sometimes we lose our momentum and just give up. The ego and the mind can only look to past experiences for solutions.

Here's my suggestion for moving past these blocks: Rely on and trust your inner voice for guidance. Every problem has a solution and every lock has a key. But first we have to learn to surrender to the outcome and trust in the flow of the Universe.

> **"**. . .*it's following the flow of the Universal Current. Like surfing a wave.***"**
>
> – Hippiebanker

This is not natural for most of us. We fight the flow rather than surrender. But you know what? When surrender happens, the way through every block appears. Now, surrender does not mean losing. Surrender is not the same as being passive. It's not giving up; it's following the flow of the Universal Current. Like surfing a wave. It's trusting in spiritual life force energy. In order to do that, we have to stay present and trust in ourselves as well. Ride the wave, and guess what? We will get to where we want to go and faster than if we were fighting against the flow. It's all about trusting that the Universe has a greater plan for us.

Once we surrender, we will come to realize that the way through every block is through love. Challenges provide us the opportunity to open our hearts wider and make a connection with our coworkers.

Our Intentions for This Week

1. **Sit with these blocks and feel the emotions.** Don't dismiss them too quickly. Sit with the emotion and really try to feel that feeling. Tell yourself, *I'm feeling angry right now. I'm feeling sad.* Whatever the emotion, let it be. Tell yourself that emotion is not who you are. It's just a temporary feeling. Let it ride out, then gently release the emotions and bless them as they go.

2. **When you are feeling out of sync, spend time outdoors and try putting your bare feet in contact with the ground.** This concept is called *earthing* or grounding. The Earth's energy is very healing. Hippies and "tree huggers" know a thing or two about reconnecting with earth. They know that Mother Nature is a giant battery that we can go to when we want to recharge and reconnect with source. Try it this week. Even if you giggle and feel like a child again, I promise this is time well spent.

3. **Try journaling.** I've recently discovered the benefits of free-style journaling. Whenever there's an issue or situation at work that I can't figure out on my own, I turn to the Universe for guidance. I'll meditate first, light some incense, then start writing in my journal. The trick is not to try and control what you're writing. Just let the ideas flow without judgment. You're the only one reading it, so don't worry about what comes out. Just keep writing whatever pops in your head and before long, it will seem like someone else

has taken charge of the pen. Don't be alarmed—that's spirit guiding you and helping you work through your blocks. Go with the flow until you feel it's time to stop. Then take a minute to re-read your thoughts. You might have been given some mighty important downloads from the Universe.

If we can change our perspective on challenges, we will realize they are actually opportunities for growth on our spiritual path. Try to surrender to the outcome and wait for the answer to be shown to you. It takes *trust*. You can do it.

Recently, I had a very challenging situation come up at work, and at first, I went right to my old default of fear and anger. The old me would stay with these emotions for weeks. They would cling to me all day and linger into the weekend as well. As I've practiced these three intentions, I've learned to release the low-level vibes and come back to my natural state of love. This particular time, I was back on track within a day.

Remember, we all fall off the path. We're learning how to get back on track quickly and live in our Light. As you commit to being a spiritual activist at work, you will start to welcome these challenges and become the go-to person when your coworkers and peers need help.

Keep shining and don't forget to "Turn off your minds, relax and float downstream. It is not dying"

Remember . . . we are all one
Namaste'

Whatever is flexible and flowing will tend to grow.
Whatever is rigid and blocked will wither and die.
– Tao Te Ching

Everything you want is on the other side of fear.
– Jack Canfield

In my defenselessness my safety lies.
– A Course in Miracles

Surrender, Let Go and Let God Work.
– Rick Warren

The wound is the place where the Light enters you.

– Rumi

Week 10

It is Time

Last week we learned about the Second Sutra of the Aquarian Age, "There is a way through every block," and how to apply it in the workplace. How did it go last week?

Did you meditate on any blocks and see them as opportunities to grow and learn?

Did you go outside and wiggle your toes in the dirt? I'll bet you haven't done that in a long time.

Or did you hug a tree?

Hopefully, your neighbors weren't watching and thought you've lost your mind . . . or maybe they joined in on the fun! Maybe you enjoyed some free-style journaling and had a few breakthroughs. The biggest question is this: *Did you surrender to the outcome?*

Surrendering is probably the hardest practice to undertake, especially if you're in a position of leadership at work—or if you are a control freak like me. You're used to controlling every situation and directing employees to your thoughts of what the outcome should look like. It takes trust to surrender to the Universe for guidance on a challenging situation or block. However, if you come to the meditation pillow with defenses down, a willingness to be open to a solution, and ask for guidance, the answer is given to you. There is a lesson there somewhere.

Remember, the world is your classroom and people are your teachers. And since you probably spend the majority of your day at work, you really could look at it this way: Your workplace is your classroom and your coworkers are your teachers.

Now on to this week's lesson. As we continue to apply the Five Sutras of the Aquarian Age to the workplace, we'll move on to the next. The Third Sutra is:

WHEN THE TIME IS ON YOU, START AND THE PRESSURE WILL BE OFF

FIRST AND FOREMOST, this sutra speaks to us directly as Lightworkers. We are asked to become teachers who can offer guidance and inspire our coworkers along in their journeys. We are being called to help light up the world and we have a lot of work to do!

I hope you can tell how passionate I am about leading through love, not fear, and about bringing that miracle mindset to the workplace. This sutra is about bringing my spirituality to work *now*—not next week, not tomorrow—

NOW. It's feeling the call to make a difference in the world . . . the world that encompasses your work life and that which is very sacred to you, your home life. Of course, it doesn't make sense that you would be a loving mother, father, daughter, son or friend at home and then when you go to work, all that you are just stops—because actually, *that's where it's needed most.*

> " *Before you know it, spirit will be infused in who you are and in every moment.* "
> – Hippiebanker

We have to step into our role, be responsible and get out of our own way. We need to be aware of our actions at work and how they affect our coworkers. Treat your coworkers like family. So when Yogi Bhajan says "Start and the pressure will be off," I believe he is saying that if you feel the calling to be a spiritual activist at work, *just start.* You don't have to have all the answers. Go to a bookstore and check out the spirituality section. A book might call to you. Read a blog or go to a metaphysical store and read up on crystals. Before you know it, spirit will be infused in who you are and in every moment. It will just naturally spill over into your work life. Watch out, I sense a Lightworker coming to a job near you!

This sutra also applies to how we handle difficult situations at work that need addressing, when we feel overwhelmed, or don't know where to begin on a project or task. It even applies to those days when you have so many little things to get done, and you don't know where to start or how to prioritize. Some people will procrastinate. Others will think of reasons why they can't handle a situation. When we procrastinate, it's usually because of the underlying emotion of fear. We fear the unknown. We don't know what the next right step is. We worry and stress about "what if this is wrong, or what if this is not going to give me the results I want?" If you continue with the mantra of "what if, what if . . ." nothing gets done. Worry and stress only causes more worry and stress. When we worry, we actually separate ourselves from our true nature, which is love, and we block our spiritually guided, life-force energy.

OUR INTENTIONS FOR THIS WEEK

1. First, stop and listen to your inner guide. Breathe, clear your mind and then take action. Just take the first step in the direction of your goal and the pressure will be off. You don't have to have a final plan just yet. Just start moving. You'll be guided to the next right action if you trust in the Universe. Think of it this way: If you want to go somewhere in your car and you don't know how to get there, if you just sit in your car in the driveway, nothing is going to happen. Start the car, take it out of "park" and put it in "drive" and *start moving.*

Think of your inner guidance as your GPS. You rely on your GPS to get you to your destination—why not rely on the Universe? Your inner guide, Source, the Universe, spirit, whatever you want to call it, knows the next right action.

We just need to trust that it will get us to our destination. Eventually, you'll get in the right lane and everything will start to flow.

Then try this: Do a temperature check on yourself. The pressure will immediately ease up; you will gain momentum to keep going; worry and stress will start to disappear; and, before long, the solution will be revealed.

2. Know you can do this. Whether you are committed to being a full-blown spiritual "I'm going to change the world" activist at work, or whether you are going to gently nudge some of your coworkers into seeing the bright side of life, just *know you can do this.*

You don't have to have ten certificates hanging on your wall to know your worth. You have all it takes within you to change the vibration in the room. All you need is a little willingness, faith in yourself and determination. And if you start a project at work and start procrastinating, repeat this sutra silently to yourself. Be the little engine that could!

3. When in doubt, pray it out. If you encounter any difficult situations at work and don't have a clear solution to the problem, I recommend handing it over to the Universe. Before you go to bed, write down what's on your mind. Just doing that will release some of the tension. Pray for a solution and hand it over to God, source or your inner guide. Prayer is a mighty useful tool. Never discount how powerful prayer can be. Before long, the answers to your prayers will miraculously appear. Trust and let go.

~

So remember, *when the time is on you, just start.* You don't have to have all the answers. You don't have to wait till you are perfect at something. You'll spend what seems like an eternity perfecting a product, your speech, how to attain your goals at work, how to start a book about bringing peace, love and spirituality to the workplace. You don't have to have every credential and you certainly don't have to have all the answers. Just believe, trust and ask for guidance. Put the car in drive. Once you get the car rolling, you'll immediately feel a weight lift off your shoulders. That's the Universe cheering you on and saying "You're off and headed towards the finish line!

. . . You've got this one!"

Remember . . . we are all one.
Namaste'

No matter how hard the past. You can always begin again.
  − Buddha

What you think, you become. What you feel, you attract.
What you imagine, you create.
– Buddha

Happiness is not determined by what's happening around you but rather by what's happening within you.

– Buddha

Peace comes from within. Do not seek it without.

– Buddha

Quiet the mind and the soul will speak.
– Buddha

Week 11

Acting from the Heart

Hello once more. We have been learning about the Five Sutras of the Aquarian Age and bringing them to life in the workplace. Last week we explored the Third Sutra, which is: *When the time is on YOU, start and the pressure will be off.* So I'll ask you:

Did you meditate on this mantra and come to realize that if we are choosing to be spiritual activists in our workplace, we don't have to have all the answers?

We don't need to have any fancy credentials—just make a decision to start. There are so many people at work who need us. They need us to be vulnerable and show them it's always best to speak the truth, even if your voice shakes. They need us to show the Light that's within all of us and help them awaken to their authentic selves.

Most people are dealing with one thing or another at

home. We all have issues and if we can help our coworkers smile during the day and help them come from a place of love, it might just spill over into their home life.

I encourage you to continue practicing the sutras going forward. You've made a commitment to being a spiritual activist. Take this responsibility seriously. People change jobs all the time these days. However, I promise you this: When you touch another person's soul, even if they leave your workplace, they will never forget you and how you made them feel.

Now, on to . . . you guessed it . . . The Fourth Sutra, which is:

UNDERSTAND THROUGH COMPASSION OR YOU WILL MISUNDERSTAND THE TIMES

WHAT IS COMPASSION and how can we apply this sutra to the workplace? Compassion means to show special kindness to those who suffer. Compassion is opening our hearts to the feelings of others without judgment. How do we do this? By acting from the heart. Now, compassion does not mean we overlook the mistakes made by our coworkers. It means we have sympathy and understanding for their difficulties and know we are not different from them.

There can be many reasons we get upset with our coworkers. We may feel we work harder than another person, or we think our solution to a problem is the best and only solution. Maybe we don't have patience with our coworkers.

Sometimes, when we move up the corporate ladder, it's easy to forget where we came from. We forget what it was like struggling to get to the next rung, and what it felt like when a coworker or boss didn't show compassion when we had to call out because we were sick. Or when it took a little longer to understand a new policy or procedure. We only remember where we are now, and we forget who and what got us to the next level.

It's ingrained in us to be logical and to hide our emotions in the workplace. The mind is held in higher regard than the heart. By tapping into the power of your heart, you will discover your ability to be compassionate.

> " *The ego will try to tell you that you are a weak leader if you live from the heart.*"
> – Hippiebanker

At first, your ego will resist it. The ego will always bring up many reasons why someone doesn't deserve your compassion. It will also try to tell you that you are a weak leader if you live from your heart. (Believe me, your ego will be relentless on this advice.) In addition, your ego will start judging others. Judgment will keep you small. Judgment is that nasty little trick the ego uses to separate us from others.

How do you feel when you judge someone? I feel tense and disconnected. It doesn't feel natural. Try to not give in to your fear-based ego. Instead of honoring your mind, live from your heart.

When we are compassionate, we shift from a *me*

mentality to a *we* mentality. And isn't that what the workplace is—a team effort?

As someone who has continuously led through love instead of fear, I will tell you this: Your heart will always lead you to a better outcome. And you know what? In return, you'll be a fierce leader!

Our Intentions for This Week

This week, when you have a situation at work and are struggling to understand another's point of view, try this exercise. It's from the book, *Resurfacing Techniques* by Harry Palmer.[3] Start with one individual. You can use this exercise for a coworker, your boss, your mentor or even a customer. Say these steps to yourself discreetly and use the person's name for each one:

Step 1: "Just like me, this person is seeking happiness in his/her life."
Step 2: "Just like me, this person is trying to avoid suffering in his/her life."
Step 3: "Just like me, this person has known sadness, loneliness & despair."
Step 4: "Just like me, this person is seeking to fill his/her needs."
Step 5: "Just like me, this person is learning about life."

> The exercises above are reprinted with permission from *ReSurfacing®: Techniques for Exploring Consciousness* by Harry Palmer. © 1994, 1997 Harry Palmer.

Afterwards, give yourself a temperature check. Now how are you feeling? Do you feel your heart opening up? Do you feel connected with that person? Step outside yourself and witness your thoughts.

∼

TO ME, THE FOURTH SUTRA is an experience of oneness. It's about speaking and feeling from your heart and connecting with your coworkers on a soul level. It's forgetting about our differences and recognizing what we have in common. We all crave attention, recognition and happiness. It's not always someone else we must show compassion for. Sometimes it's ourselves. We need to let ourselves off the hook and not be so judgmental and ready to put ourselves down. Easier said than done, you may say; but if we practice this week, starting with one person (or ourselves) and continue throughout the week, it will become easier to experience oneness through compassion.

This week, keep your heart open as you approach people and challenges. Try to resist the urge to go into judgment or to go into your ego and separate yourself from others. Remember to look into your coworker's eyes and see the Light that shines brightly in all of us. It's there. All that you need to develop compassion lies within you. Start your practice today. The payoff is enormous.

Remember . . . we are all one.
Namaste'

Be the change you want to see in the world.
– Gandhi

*Happiness is when what you think, what you say,
and what you do are in harmony.*

– Gandhi

The weak can never forgive.
Forgiveness is the attribute of the strong.

– Gandhi

My life is my message.
   – Gandhi

The best way to find yourself
is to lose yourself in the service of others.
– Gandhi

WEEK 12

ONE LOVE, ONE TRIBE

THESE LAST FEW WEEKS we've learned about applying the Five Sutras of the Aquarian Age to the workplace. Last week we worked on the Fourth Sutra, which is "*Understand through compassion or you will misunderstand the times.*" So I'll ask:

How was it last week trying to show compassion to your coworkers? It's easy showing compassion when everything is going just swimmingly, isn't it? But how do we continue to be compassionate when we are just not jiving with our coworkers?

Did you practice the five steps from last week? "Just like me, this person is learning about life." This brings you back to love, which is non-judgmental, doesn't it?

It brought me to my mantra . . . *we are all one.*

~

We started this journey because we are Lightworkers and spiritual activists. We are here to shed our Light on a place where typically there is no light. Where people come, do their job (not happily most of the time) and go home. They might bring spirituality to their home life. They might meditate, practice mindfulness, and read positive affirmations; however, not at work. We signed on to "be the Light" through good times and bad (kind of like a marriage). The test is really through the bad times—when you don't *feel* like being the Light.

How can we show compassion when we are stuck in our egos, believing we have to prove we are right, or our way is the only way?

Hopefully, last week you practiced compassion and felt a heaviness lift. It's quite a burden to continue being judgmental and uncaring. Once you practice leading through your heart, you will undoubtedly feel lighter. The weight is lifted and once you get that high-vibe feeling, you won't want to go back to those low-level vibes of blame, hostility and resentment. Shake them off and send them on their way.

Speaking of vibes, we are ready to tackle our last sutra, which is:

Vibrate the Cosmos and the Cosmos Shall Clear the Earth

What is the *cosmos* and why should be vibrate with it? What path is it going to clear for us and where does that path lead? Well, in our context, the cosmos is the Universe or whatever you want to call it: God, the Universe, Source, Spirit or your inner guide.

So here's a secret: Everything has a vibration. The entire Universe is a vibration of energy. Every minute of the day, we are all vibrating on an emotional level, cellular level and a spiritual level. Mind . . . Body . . . Soul. Everything that exists has a vibrational frequency. We vibrate frequency through our thoughts, words, actions, emotions and feelings. We are either vibrating in harmony with the Universe or disharmony with the Universe. High vibes or low vibes. So, when Yogi Bhajan is saying "Vibrate the cosmos," he's clearly saying *vibrate at a higher frequency.* Those frequencies are that of love, compassion and kindness.

When we vibrate in harmony with the cosmos, everything falls into place. Whatever vibrational frequency we are on will draw a "match" into our life. If you've heard of the *Law of Attraction,* then you know this: You draw in what you think about. It will manifest in your life. What we put out into the Universe we receive back, like a *boomerang.*

Now, what about clearing the path? When you vibrate at a higher frequency, your path becomes clear. You're aligned with your higher self. Your thoughts are clear and you can make sound decisions. Think of it this way: It's like traveling on the highway. (I know, another car analogy.) When you are vibrating at a lower frequency, you're stuck in traffic. Think hot, humid day, with no A/C in the car. You're blocked from getting to your destination. When you're vibrating at a higher frequency, it's smooth sailing. No stop lights. No cars in your way. You have the music blasting. Your favorite song is on; there are beautiful majestic mountains on one side, the clear ocean on the other side. The top is down; your hair is flying. It's a magical feeling! Things just fall into place and guess what? *Miracles happen naturally!* Count on them!

OUR INTENTIONS FOR THIS WEEK . . . AND GOING FORWARD.

1. First and foremost, the most important thing you can do is meditate daily. I am a firm believer in mediating every morning. Call on the ascended masters, your spirit guides and your beautiful angels. Sit in silence and ask for guidance and protection. Then ask the Universe "How can I be of service today?" Be open to that guidance and trust in the outcome. It's life changing, I promise. And as always, come from a place of love. Love makes people believe in themselves and feel valued, and allows them to have the same effect on others. In any situation you encounter at work, ask "What would love do?" Love is your natural state of being. You'll feel more in tune with yourself if you come from a place of love. And guess what the outcome will be? An awesome life filled with JOY and ABUNDANCE!

2. Be aware of your words, actions and tone of your voice. When you are talking to a coworker, employee, your supervisor ask yourself this:

Would I talk to my mother or father like this?

Would I use these words and tone with someone I honor and respect?

If not, Stop . . . *Breathe.*

When you ask yourself that question, it brings you back in the now.

Just like we talked about last week, we are all learning about life. We are all on a spiritual journey, and deep down, we are all spiritual teachers. We all have something to share. The trick is to find your voice and speak your truth gently. Practice compassion, lead through your heart and we will get back to that place where *love is all you need.*

3. Practice gratitude. Take time each day to be grateful for your job. Be grateful for your paycheck. Be grateful for the people you are surrounded by at work. Like I mentioned before, think of your job as your classroom and your coworkers as your teachers. People come into your life as assignments to help you grow spiritually. There is a *soul lesson* and a *soul purpose* every day. If we can step back and not let our egos take control by placing blame and judgment, we can be grateful for all experiences.

Keep a gratitude journal just for work. At the end of the day, take time to journal what went well and find one thing you are grateful for. If you take nothing else away from this book, take away the importance of a daily practice of gratitude. Even if you have one of those horrible days at work where everything is falling apart, try and find a silver lining and write it down. "Wow, today was awful. Nothing went according to plan. I couldn't get any of my tasks accomplished. Well, at least my hair looked good today!" One small piece of gratitude will make you smile and bring you back to that super cool highway where you're singing at the top of your lungs.

∼

WE CHOOSE WHO WE ARE by what we put out in the Universe—every minute, by our thoughts, words and actions. If we look inward and find ourselves uncomfortable and feel we are blocked, the Universe is telling us we are out of alignment with our truth. Our truth is *we are Love.*

Once we are aligned with our natural state of love, the cosmos shall clear the path, helping us achieve all that we want. To vibrate in harmony with the cosmos is to know that we are all in this together. One Love. One Tribe.

Live your life as a demonstration of this truth.

Remember . . . we are all one.
Namaste'

1. Just for today, I will not be angry.

* The quotes for these five pages of journaling, use the five principles of Reiki.

2. Just for today, I will not worry.

3. Just for today, I will be grateful.

4. Just for today, I will do my work honestly.

5. Just for today, I will be kind to every living thing.

AFTERWORD

IN THE BEGINNING of this book, I revealed that I don't consider myself to be an expert on the subject of spirituality. I just know I'm being divinely guided to help spread the message that peace, love and spirituality has its place in the workplace.

There was a time when I thought, in order to be an effective manager, I would have to lead with an iron fist and intimidate others. I tried to get results by infusing fear into my coworkers. It didn't take long to realize that not only was that path ineffective, but more importantly, it made me feel horrible inside! This was not the way I wanted to lead, nor the way I wanted to live my life. Since then, I've made the commitment to lead through love, not fear. Now mind you, this commitment takes small, daily steps and practice. It takes patience and the ability to rebound when you fall off the spiritual path. Remember, it's not about staying in that positive vibe 100% of the time, it's recognizing when you veer off and having the tools and intentions to get back on track to that groovy state of love, where your aura will be shining brightly.

There are several tips and concepts I've touched upon in this book and I encourage you to read more about them if you feel inclined to do so. Reading more about these concepts will give you fulfillment and confidence in your role as a Lightworker. In my experience, two of these principles are the initial stepping stones of a spiritual activist. Those are the daily practice of meditation and gratitude.

A morning meditation will help start your day off with a positive intention, and a nightly gratitude affirmation will end your day on a high note. During your morning meditation, ask for guidance on any blocks you have encountered at work and you will be shown the next right action. Then, ask the Universe these thought-provoking words from *A Course in Miracles*:[5]

> *What would You have me do?*
> *Where would You have me go?*
> *What would You have me say, and to whom?*

Keep these words close to you during your day and refer to them often. I've found them to be comforting in times of stress. They've kept me close to my inner world where I feel safe and secure. Then at night, take time to reflect on your day and write a few sentences on what you're grateful for. It doesn't have to be earth shattering. Just be grateful for the simple things in life, those sweet intangibles that are the cornerstone of a life well lived. These are simple steps you can do going forward to ensure you continue on your spiritual path. I also encourage you to re-read this book, as well as your notes, and look at where you've made the biggest improvement, e.g., Does one week stand out as a game changer? Do you want to take that week and make it your mission to instill that concept or intention into your work life as well as your home life?

There are so many spiritual practices you can incorporate into your life. Maybe find one that intrigues you and read everything you can on that subject. Start teaching it to your coworkers on a deeper level. Remember, the more you teach, the more you learn.

My hope with this guide is that it will help us to recognize we are connected by one spirit and we are all in this together. We are here to serve, uplift and help one another. We can apply this principle to our coworkers and make life at work a unique and beautiful experience.

Be the person that allows others to shine and help them on their spiritual journey. If you start living from this sacred space, you'll find life to be a miraculous experience.

The most important piece of advice I can leave you with is this: Don't be afraid to step fully into your role as a Lightworker. There is a shift happening on this planet and we are experiencing a need for more spiritual teachers—people to show others that we are all connected to one another and to a higher being. If you feel that calling, know that you are being guided to answer the call. We need you!

You are here to fulfill your divine purpose and help bring light into the world. We are all here for a reason. Each one of us has a talent that we are meant to share with the world, and we are all spiritual teachers in our own right. We each have a unique gift; if we can go within and see what it is, we can help spread peace and love to everyone we meet and bring those concepts to the workplace. Once you've awakened to your true purpose, your life will forever be changed.

∼

I've accepted my role as Hippiebanker. Now I'll ask you this . . . what is *your* role? Go out there and shine. Be the light. Unabashedly. Unapologetically. Relentlessly.

I hope this little guide has served you well. I hope you have enjoyed the last 12 weeks and that you have found this book to be informative and fun.

I honor your journey and I send you love.

Remember . . . we are all one.
Namaste'

Acknowledgments

To my coworkers, employees and mentors: I have learned something from everyone I've met at work. You have all made me into a better manager, better leader, and most importantly better person.

To my family and friends: Thank you for reading my blogs, "liking" my posts, and listening to me over and over about my mission in life! I appreciate all you've done to help my little idea evolve into this book.

To my daughters, Arianna and Carissa: This book is for you. Never stop dreaming.

To Gabby Bernstein and her husband, Zach Rocklin: Thank you for your inspiring story that has propelled me into a new chapter in my life. Gabby, I value your work immensely and hope to awaken others with this book as you've awakened me. I am proud to call myself a full-fledged Spirit Junkie.

To my cover artist, Emanuel Vinatoru: Thank you for bringing me to life.

To my publisher and editor, Denise of Six Degrees Publishing Group: Thank you for taking a chance on me and believing in me. Your support, encouragement and continued guidance have meant the world to me. I am blessed to have found you.

Last but not least, thank you to my co-creator of this book: My inner guide, spirit, source, the Universe, God. I was divinely guided to write this book and during the course of my writing have found an inner peace that I have been looking for all my life. I am forever grateful for this opportunity.

"Silence tells me secretly . . . everything"

REFERENCES

INTRODUCTION
[1] Angel Therapy ® Doreen Virtue. "8 Traits of Lightworkers," October 23, 2014, http://www.angeltherapy.com/blog/8-traits-lightworkers (accessed July 22 2015)

WEEK 3
[2] Oswald, Andrew J, Eugenio Proto and Daniel Sgroi.2015 Happiness and productivity, *Journal of Labor Economics*, 33:no 4 (forthcoming October, 2015)

WEEK 6
[3]Williamson, Marianne. *A Return to Love* New York: HarperCollins, 1992

WEEK 11:
[4]Palmer, Harry. *ReSurfacing®: Techniques for Exploring Consciousness* by Harry Palmer. 1994, 1997 (Avatar®, ReSurfacing® and Stars Edge International® are registered service marks licensed to Star's Edge, Inc. For more information: www.avatarEPC.com)

AFTERWORD
[5]Foundation for Inner Peace, Inc. *A Course in Miracles* "Workbook For Students", Part I, Lesson 71, Second Edition © 1975, 1985, 1992, Novato, CA Foundation for Inner Peace, Inc., 1992

HIPPIEBANKER'S LIST OF
RECOMMENDED READING

(Listed by author alphabetically)

1. Bernstein, Gabrielle. *May Cause Miracles*. NY: Crown Publishing/Harmony Books, 2013

2. Byrne, Rhonda. *The Secret*. NY: Atria Books/ Beyond Words, 2006

3. Chopra, Deepak. *Ageless Body Timeless Mind*. NY: Three Rivers Press, 1993

4. Coehlo, Paulo. *The Alchemist*. NY: HarperOne, 2010

5. Dooley, Mike. *Manifesting Change*. NY: Atria Books/ Beyond Words, 2010

6. Hicks, Ester and Jerry Hicks. *Ask and It is Given*. Carlsbad, CA: Hay House, 2004

7. Foundation for Inner Peace, Inc. *A Course in Miracles*. Novato, CA: Foundation for Inner Peace, 1992

8. Virtue, Doreen. *Daily Guidance from your Angels* Oracle Cards. Carlsbad, CA: Hay House, 2006

9. Walsch, Neale Donald. *Conversations with God*. NY: G.P. Putnam's Sons, Penguin Putnam, Inc., 1995

10. Williamson, Marianne. *A Return to Love*. NY: HarperCollins, 1992

ABOUT THE AUTHOR

THROUGHOUT HER CAREER, Camille has always believed in bringing peace, love and spirituality to the workplace and in the universal truth that we are all one. She's on a mission to bring that mindset to everyone she meets, both personally and professionally.

Camille's philosophy of continuously pushing aside fear and instead leading through love, while infusing spirituality into all her meetings and daily coaching sessions, has won her several awards in profitability, and contributed to uplifting customer, employee and coworker experiences throughout her career as a banker and branch manager. Camille can't help but bring what she calls her "hippie-dippie nature" to work with her each day. Many of her coworkers and peers have been treated to angel card readings, learned to see their own aura, and have started their days with the intention to "put it out in the Universe."

Although Camille will forever be a "flower child" from New York at heart, she now resides in Orlando, Florida where she is close to her two greatest achievements: her daughters Arianna and Carissa. Connect with Camille at :

www.hippiebanker.com

VISIT CAMILLE'S AUTHOR PAGE
www.SixDegreesPublishing.com

CPSIA information can be obtained at www.ICGtesting.com
Printed in the USA
LVOW07s1324010915

452375LV00001B/19/P

9 781942 497080